Igor Sukhin

Chess Camp

Volume 3: Checkmates with Many Pieces

MONGOOSE
Press

Publisher: Mongoose Press
1005 Boylston Street, Suite 324
Newton Highlands, MA 02461
info@mongoosepress.com
www.MongoosePress.com
ISBN: 9781936277094
Library of Congress Control Number: 2010932524
Distributed to the trade by National Book Network
custserv@nbnbooks.com, 800-462-6420
For all other sales inquiries please contact the publisher.

Editor: Jorge Amador
Typesetting: Frisco Del Rosario
Cover Design: Al Dianov
First English edition
0 987654321

Contents

Note for Coaches, Parents, Teachers, and Trainers

By solving the problems in the first volume of this series, students reinforced their basic knowledge of the rules of the game and got a feel for the relative strengths of the pieces. By solving the problems in the second collection, students acquired their first skills at checkmating the king, and learned to quickly give mate in one in simple positional setups.

With the problems in the third collection, we aim to: 1) help students to see patterns in multi-piece positions in the opening and the middlegame; 2) teach students to use important tactical tools such as pins, discovered checks, and double checks to deliver mate; 3) familiarize them with the typical mating scenarios that arise no later than the 16th move of the game in various chess openings – primarily in those that beginners play at first (mainly the open and half-open games); 4) teach them to develop a feel for the smallest changes in the position of the pieces (to this end, we offer pairs of middlegame and endgame situations in which a slight difference in the initial position leads to different mechanisms for achieving mate); and 5) provide practice in giving mate in six- and seven-piece pawn, minor-piece and major-piece endings.

Mate-in-one problems are still an underestimated theme in the training of novice chessplayers. The inability to quickly find an opportunity to give mate in one in any position has a negative effect on a player's development. The majority of modern games end with both players short on time (in time trouble), and in those conditions the one whose skill at giving mate in one has become automatic enjoys a serious advantage. But not knowing just one of the typical mating setups, or being unable to see it in a complicated piece arrangement, often leads to defeat even for the experienced player.

Mate in One in the Opening
Approaching the Opening
Two Pieces Against a Whole Army

White to move: Black has all of his troops on the board, and aside from the king, White has just one piece. But this piece turns out to be stronger than the whole enemy army.

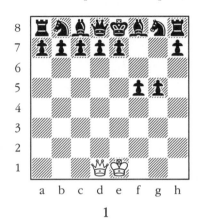

1

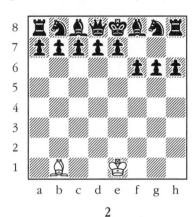

2

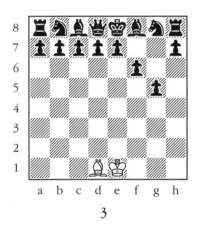

3

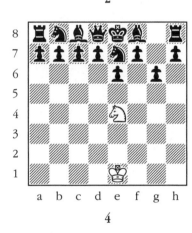

4

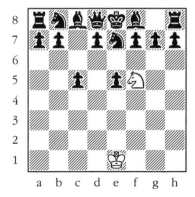

5

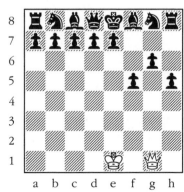

6

Two Pieces Against a Whole Army

Black to move.

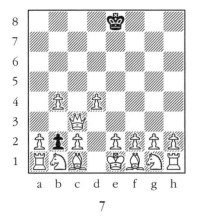

7

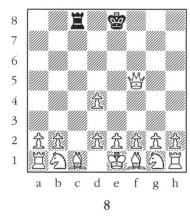

8

9

10

11

12

Three Pieces Against a Whole Army

White to move: Besides the king, White only has two pieces, and Black has his whole army frozen in its starting position. White mates him, and there are two ways to do it in each position.

13

14

15

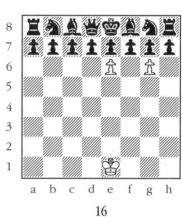

16

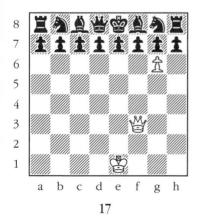

17

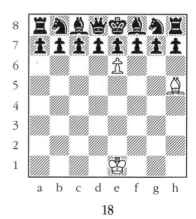

18

Three Pieces Against a Whole Army

Black to move.

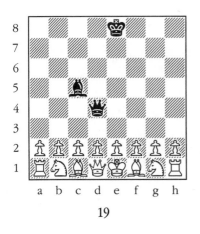

19

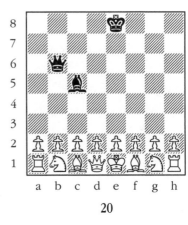

20

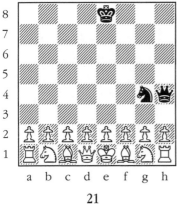

21

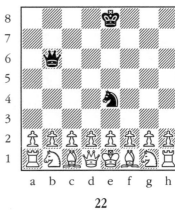

22

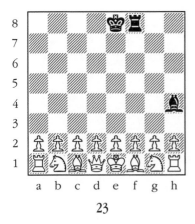

23

24

Strength in Numbers

White to move: All of White's pieces are still on their starting squares.
How to win in one move?

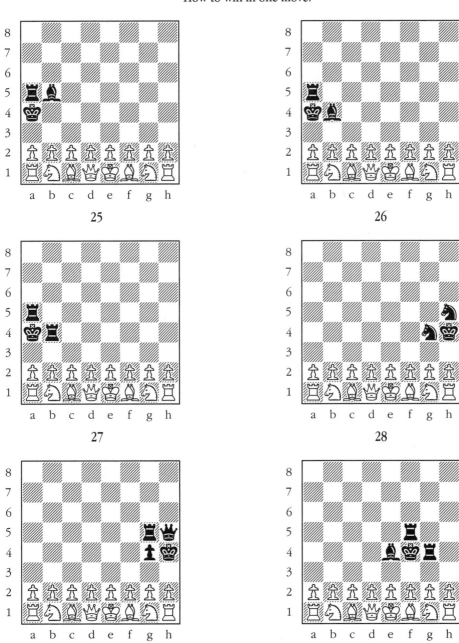

25

26

27

28

29

30

Strength in Numbers

Black to move.

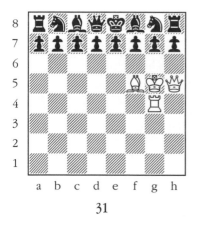

31

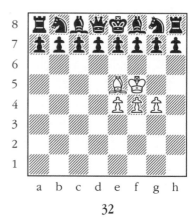

32

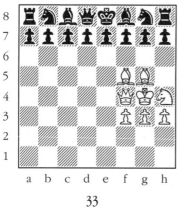

33

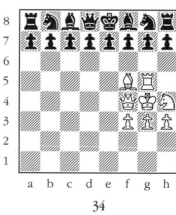

34

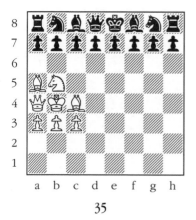

35

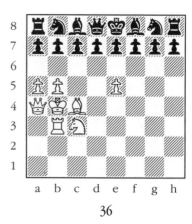

36

Silly Games
Catastrophe on Move 3

Black to move.

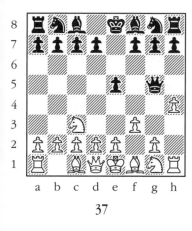

37

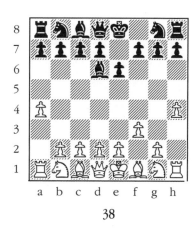

38

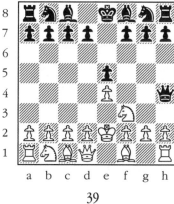

39

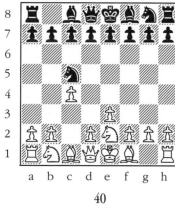

40

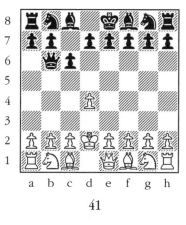

41

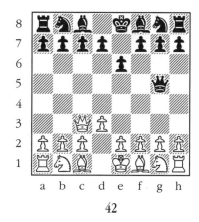

42

Catastrophe on Move 3

White to move.

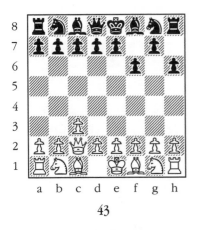

43

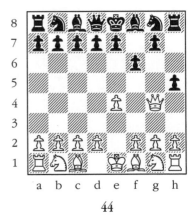

44

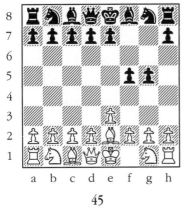

45

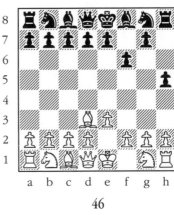

46

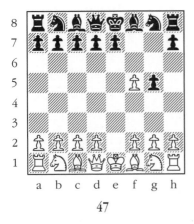

47

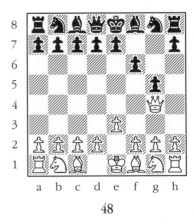

48

Catastrophe on Move 3

Black to move: For some reason, White's king has come out to the third rank. Punish him!

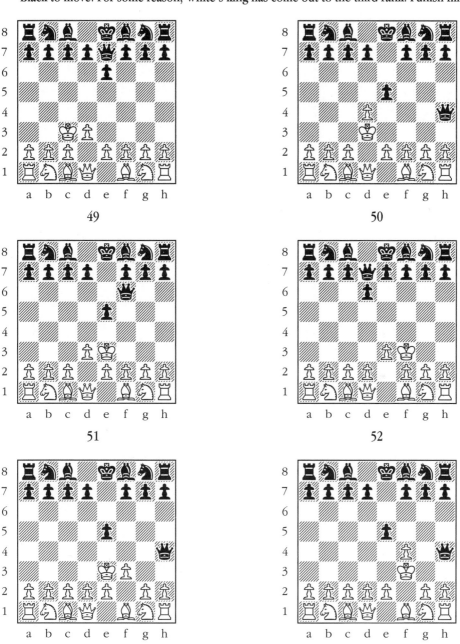

49

50

51

52

53

54

Copycats

White to move: Black wants to draw the game by copying White's moves. Punish him!

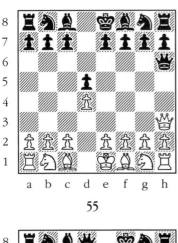

55

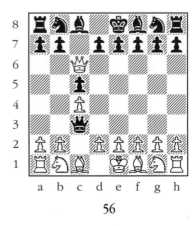

56

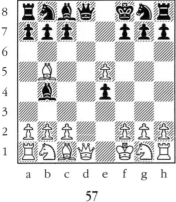

57

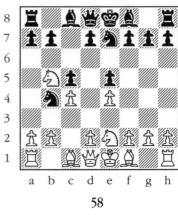

58

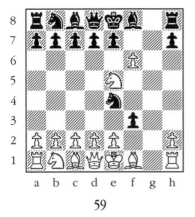

59

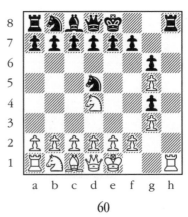

60

Open Games
The Opening Variation 1. e4 e5 2. ♕h5

White to move.

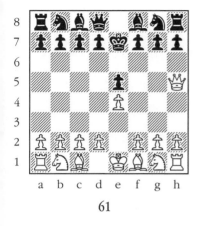

61

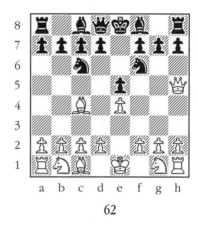

62

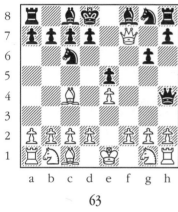

63

64

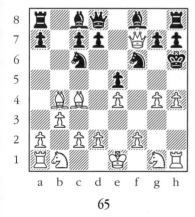

65

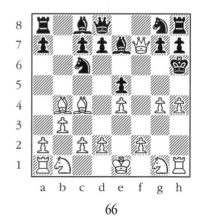

66

The Opening Variation

1. e4 e5 2. ♕h5

Black to move.

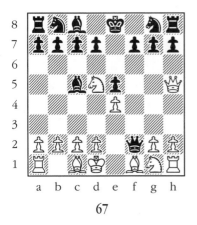

67

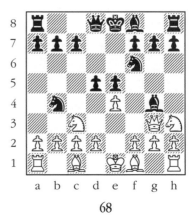

68

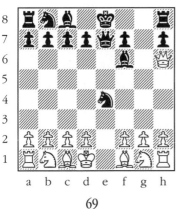

69

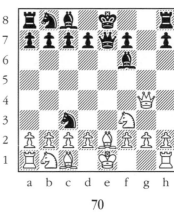

70

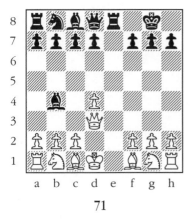

71

72

King's Gambit

1. e4 e5 2. f4

White to move.

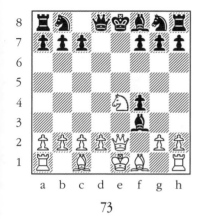

73

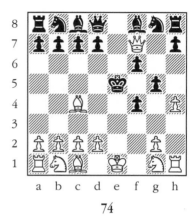

74

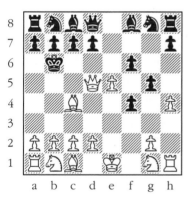

75

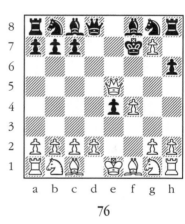

76

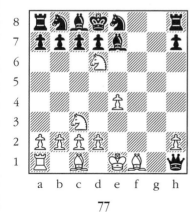

77

78

King's Gambit

1. e4 e5 2. f4

Black to move.

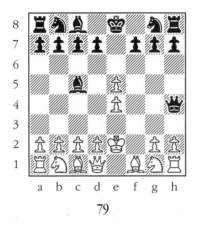

79

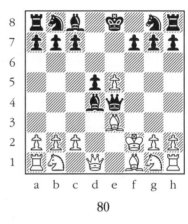

80

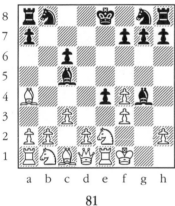

81

82

83

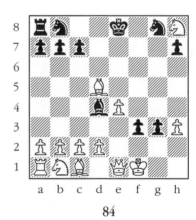

84

Center Game

1. e4 e5 2. d4

White to move.

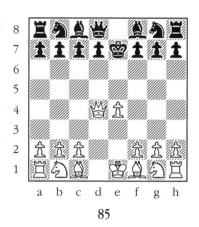

85

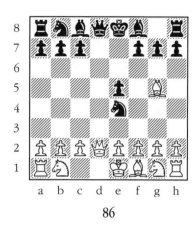

86

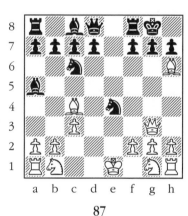

87

88

89

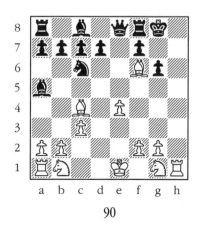

90

Danish Gambit

1. e4 e5 2. d4 exd4 3. c3

White to move.

91

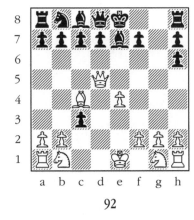

92

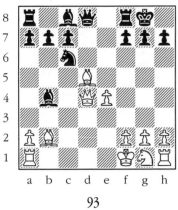

93

94

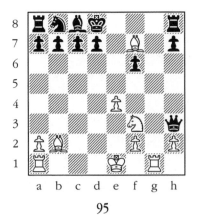

95

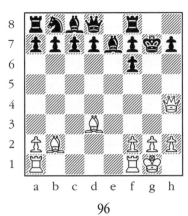

96

Bishop's Opening

1. e4 e5 2. ♗c4

White to move.

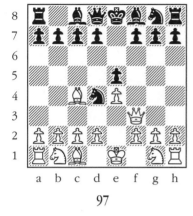

97

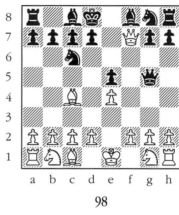

98

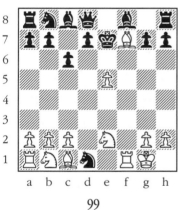

99

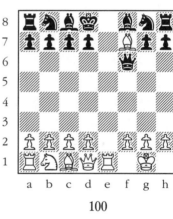

100

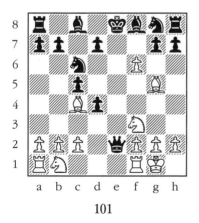

101

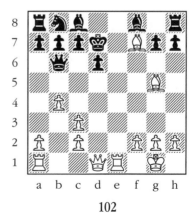

102

Vienna Game

1. e4 e5 2. ♘c3

White to move.

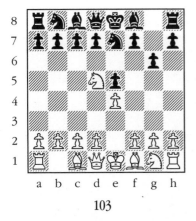

103

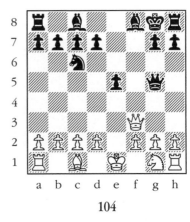

104

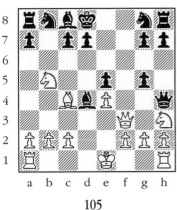

105

106

107

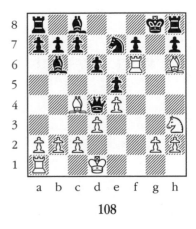

108

Vienna Game

1. e4 e5 2. ♘c3

Black to move.

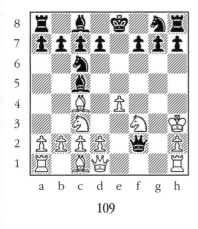

109

110

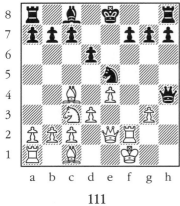

111

112

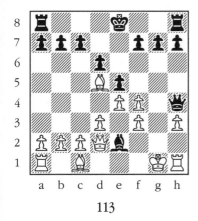

113

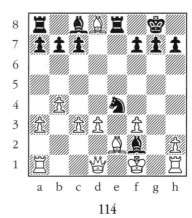

114

Damiano's Defense

1. e4 e5 2. ♘f3 f6

White to move.

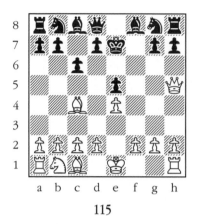

115

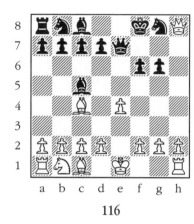

116

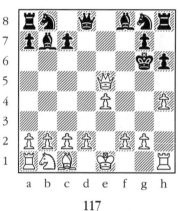

117

118

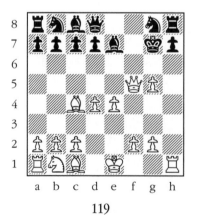

119

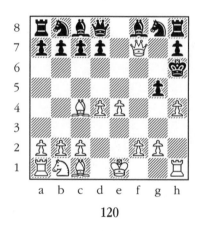

120

Latvian Gambit

1. e4 e5 2. ♘f3 f5

White to move.

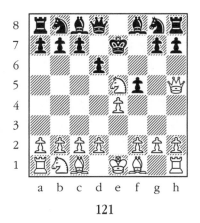

121

122

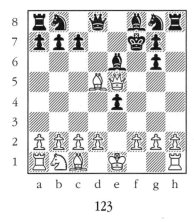

123

124

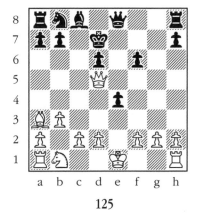

125

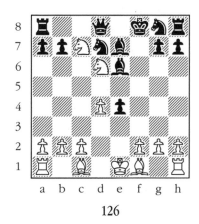

126

Latvian Gambit

1. e4 e5 2. ♘f3 f5

Black to move.

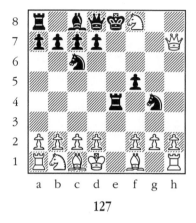

127

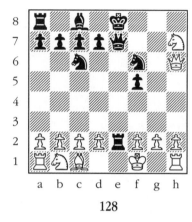

128

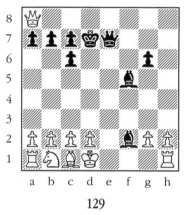

129

130

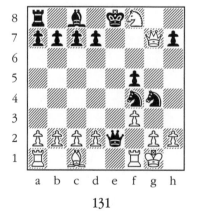

131

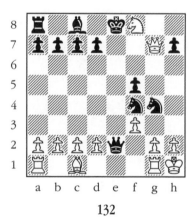

132

Philidor's Defense
1. e4 e5 2. ♘f3 d6

White to move.

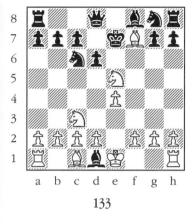

133

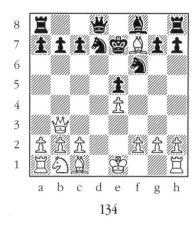

134

135

136

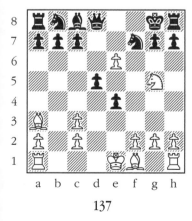

137

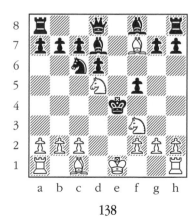

138

Petroff's Defense
1. e4 e5 2. ♘f3 ♘f6

White to move.

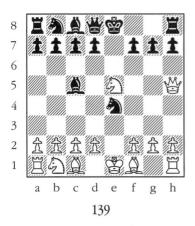

139

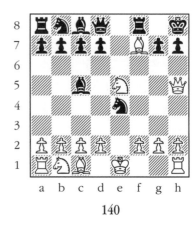

140

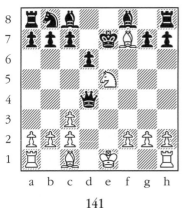

141

142

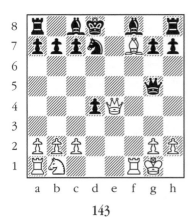

143

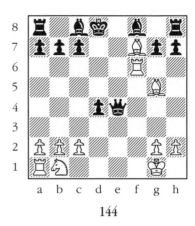

144

Scotch Game

1. e4 e5 2. ♘f3 ♘c6 3. d4

White to move.

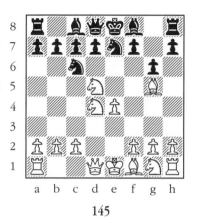

145

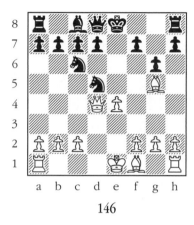

146

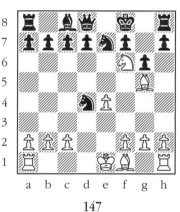

147

148

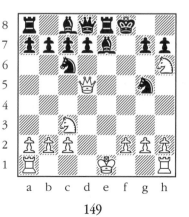

149

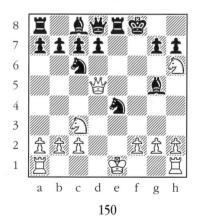

150

Göring Gambit

1. e4 e5 2. ♘f3 ♘c6 3. d4 exd4 4. c3

White to move.

151

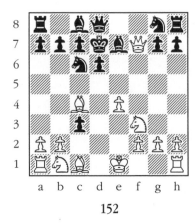

152

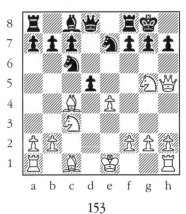

153

154

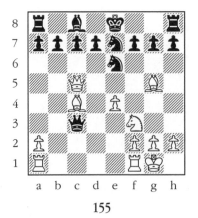

155

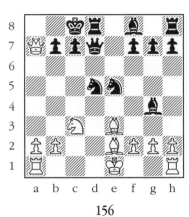

156

Ponziani's Opening
1. e4 e5 2. ♘f3 ♘c6 3. c3

White to move.

157

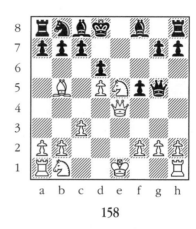

158

159

160

161

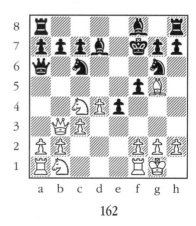

162

Two Knights' Defense

1. e4 e5 2. ♘f3 ♘c6 3. ♗c4 ♘f6

Black to move.

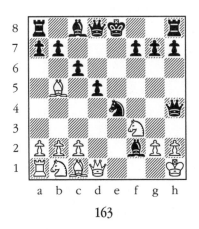

163

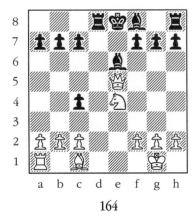

164

165

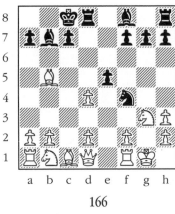

166

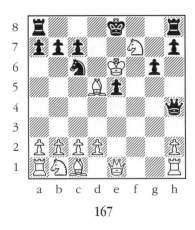

167

168

Giuoco Piano

1. e4 e5 2. ♘f3 ♘c6 3. ♗c4 ♗c5

White to move.

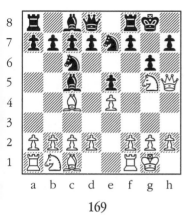

169

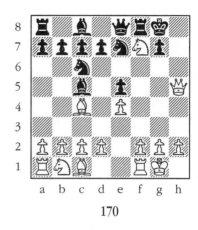

170

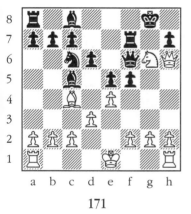

171

172

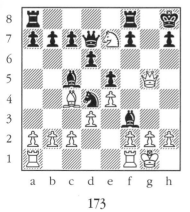

173

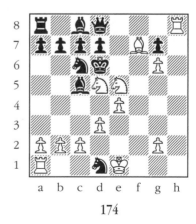

174

Giuoco Piano

1. e4 e5 2. ♘f3 ♘c6 3. ♗c4 ♗c5

Black to move.

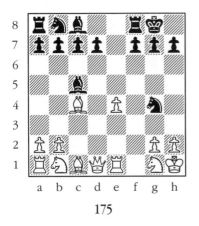

175

176

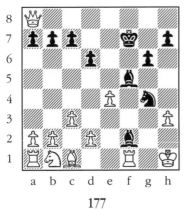

177

178

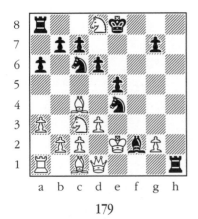

179

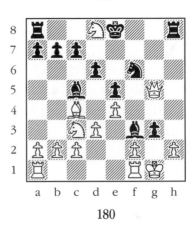

180

Evans Gambit

1. e4 e5 2. ♘f3 ♘c6 3. ♗c4 ♗c5 4. b4

White to move.

181

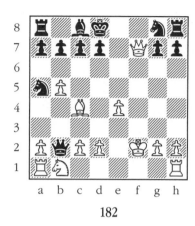

182

183

184

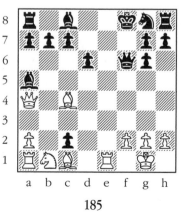

185

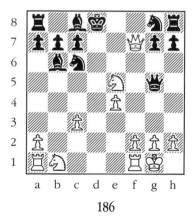

186

37

Ruy López

1. e4 e5 2. ♞f3 ♞c6 3. ♝b5

White to move.

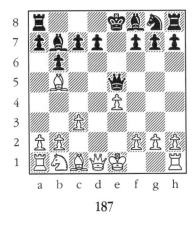

187

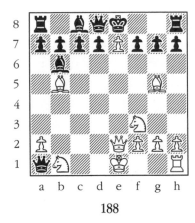

188

189

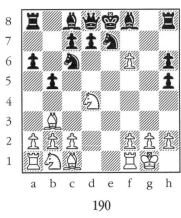

190

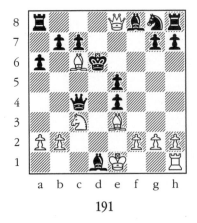

191

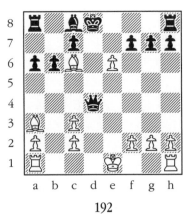

192

Ruy López
1. e4 e5 2. ♘f3 ♘c6 3. ♗b5

Black to move.

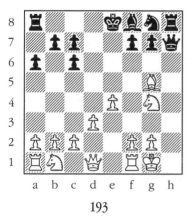

193

194

195

196

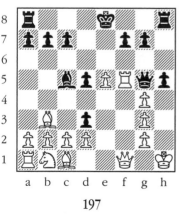

197

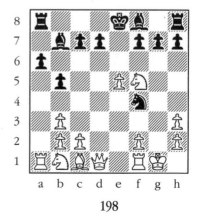

198

Semi-Open Games
Scandinavian Defense 1. e4 d5
White to move.

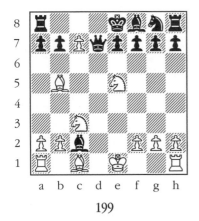

199

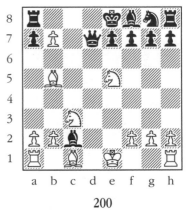

200

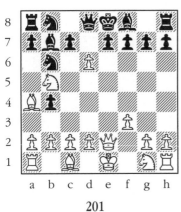

201

202

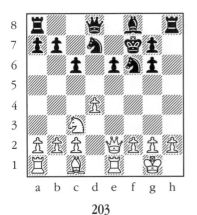

203

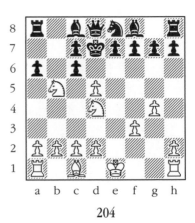

204

Scandinavian Defense

1. e4 d5

Black to move.

205

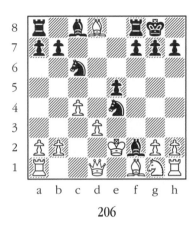

206

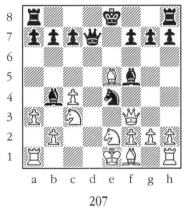

207

208

209

210

Alekhine's Defense

1. e4 ♞f6

White to move.

211

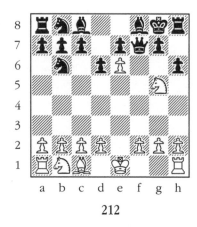

212

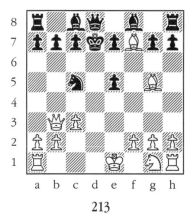

213

214

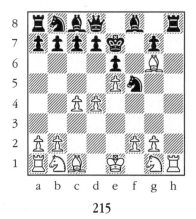

215

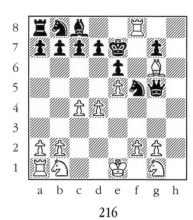

216

Alekhine's Defense

1. e4 ♘f6

Black to move.

217

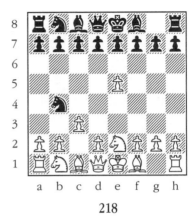

218

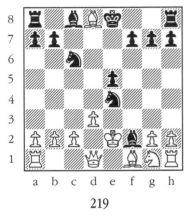

219

220

221

222

French Defense

1. e4 e6

White to move.

223

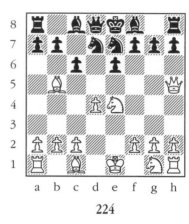

224

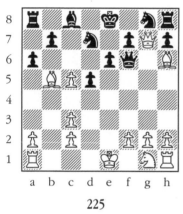

225

226

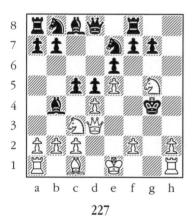

227

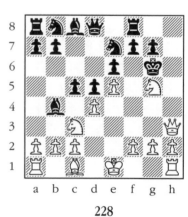

228

French Defense

1. e4 e6

Black to move.

229

230

231

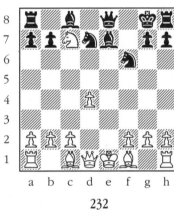

232

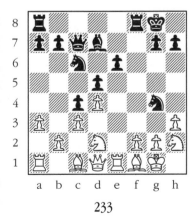

233

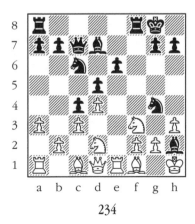

234

Caro-Kann Defense

1. e4 c6

White to move.

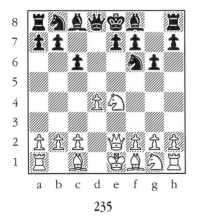

235

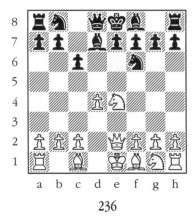

236

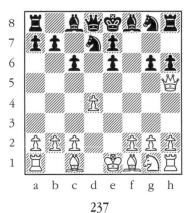

237

238

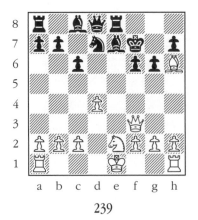

239

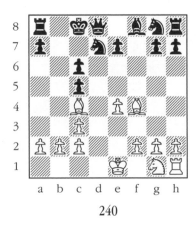

240

Pirc Defense

1. e4 d6

White to move.

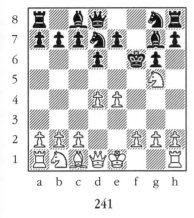

241

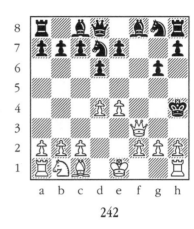

242

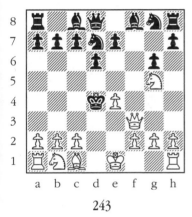

243

244

245

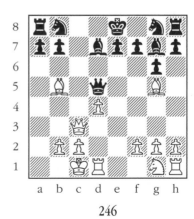

246

47

Owen's Defense

1. e4 b6

White to move.

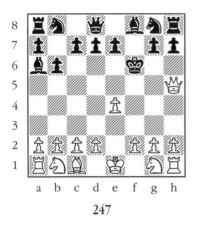

247

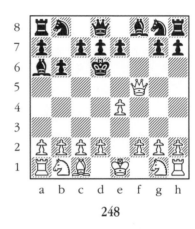

248

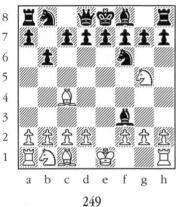

249

250

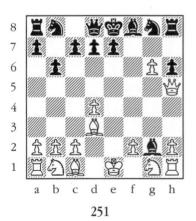

251

252

Closed Games
Bird's Opening 1. f4

Black to move.

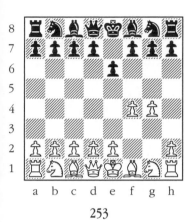

253

254

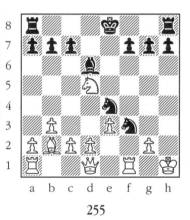

255

256

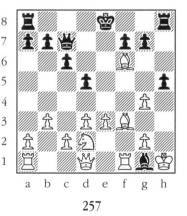

257

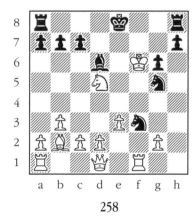

258

From's Gambit

1. f4 e5

Black to move.

259

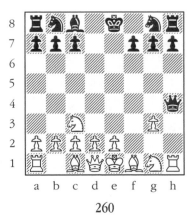

260

261

262

263

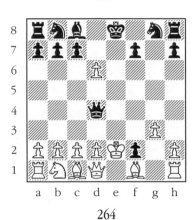

264

Dutch Defense

1. d4 f5

White to move.

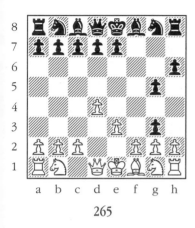

265

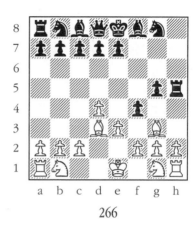

266

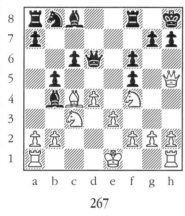

267

268

269

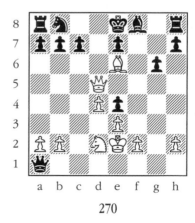

270

Queen's Gambit

1. d4 d5 2. c4

White to move.

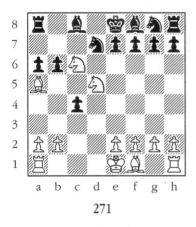

271

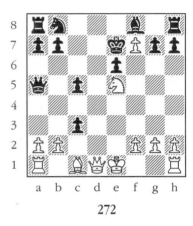

272

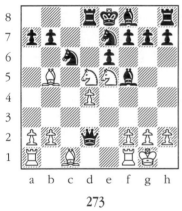

273

274

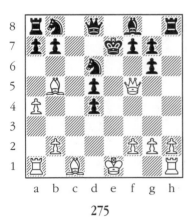

275

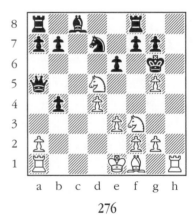

276

Albin Countergambit
1. d4 d5 2. c4 e5

Black to move.

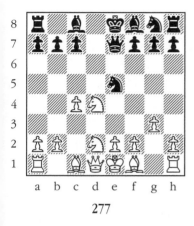

277

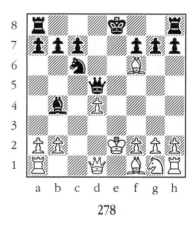

278

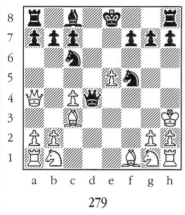

279

280

281

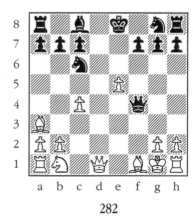

282

Budapest Gambit

1. d4 ♞f6 2. c4 e5

Black to move.

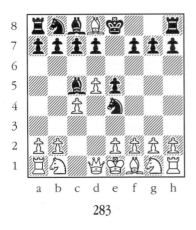

283

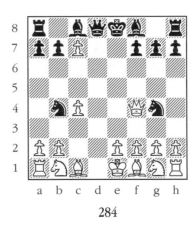

284

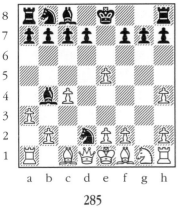

285

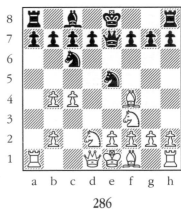

286

287

288

Mate in One in the Middlegame
Pins

White to move.

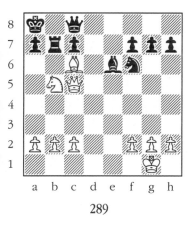

289

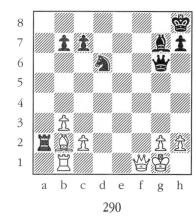

290

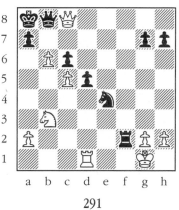

291

292

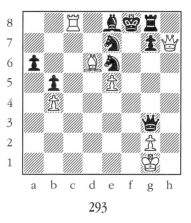

293

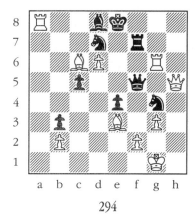

294

Pins

Black to move.

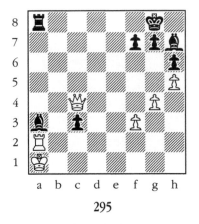

295

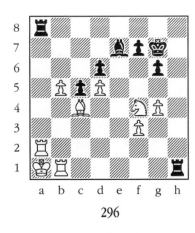

296

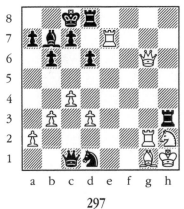

297

298

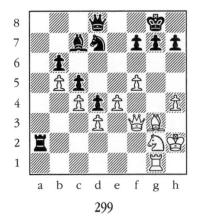

299

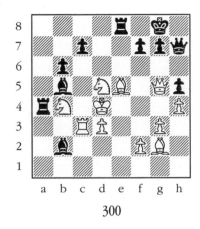

300

Silly Pin Positions

White to move.

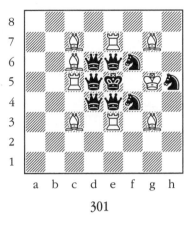

301

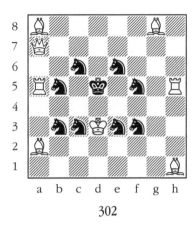

302

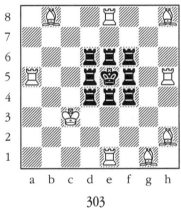

303

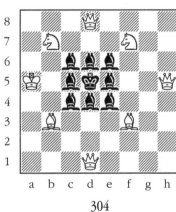

304

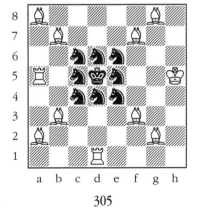

305

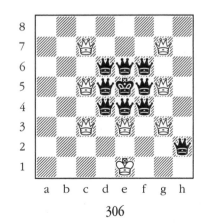

306

Double Check

White to move.

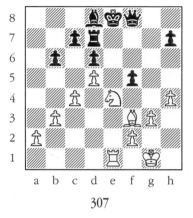

307

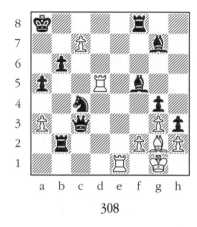

308

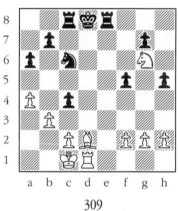

309

310

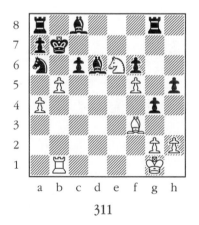

311

312

Double Check

Black to move.

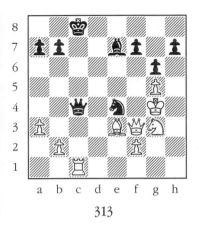

313

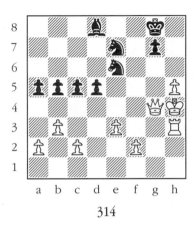

314

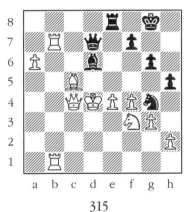

315

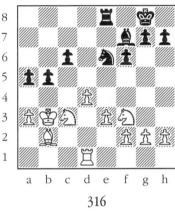

316

317

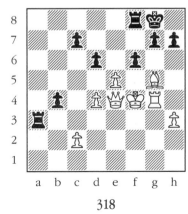

318

Discovered Check

White to move.

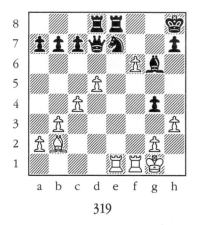

319

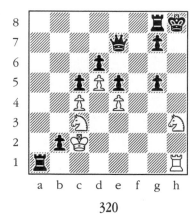

320

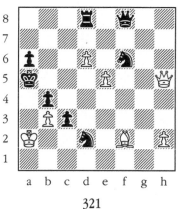

321

322

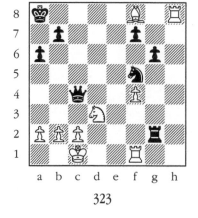

323

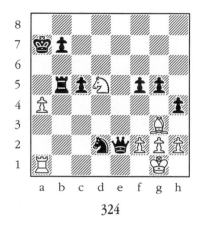

324

Discovered Check

Black to move.

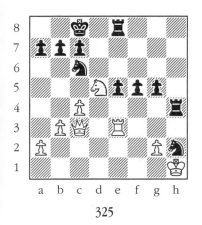

325

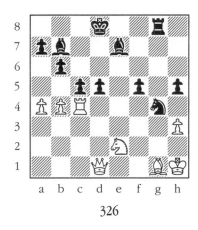

326

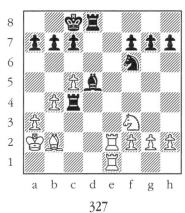

327

328

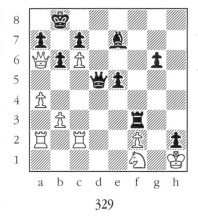

329

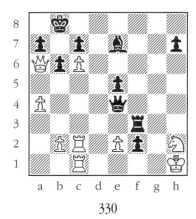

330

Attacking the Kingside Castled Position

Black to move.

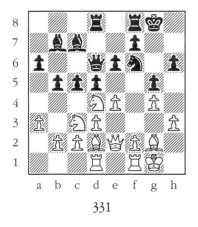

331

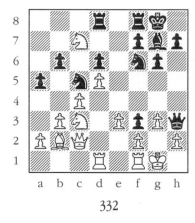

332

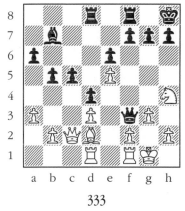

333

334

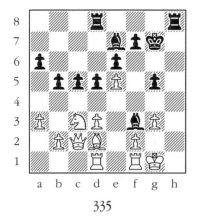

335

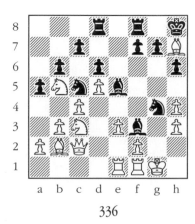

336

Attacking the Queenside Castled Position

White to move.

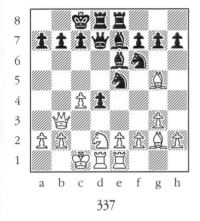

337

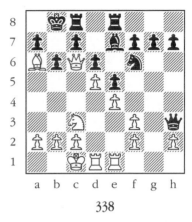

338

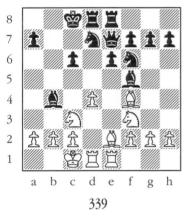

339

340

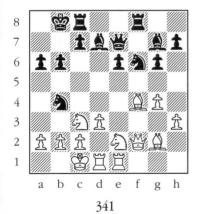

341

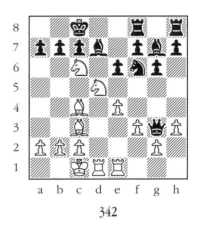

342

Attacking an Uncastled King

White to move.

343

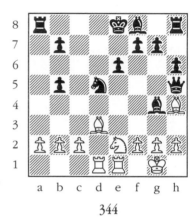

344

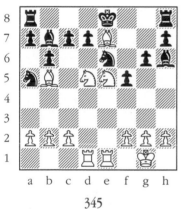

345

346

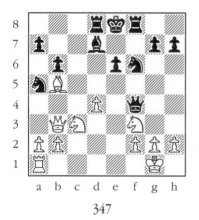

347

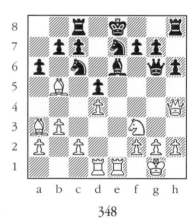

348

Checkmate as a Defense from Check

White to move: Black announced check and thought that it was mate, but White wins.

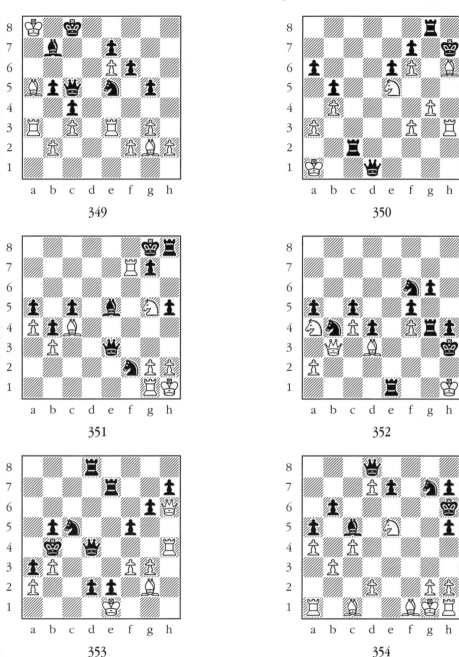

349

350

351

352

353

354

Checkmate as a Defense from Double Check

Black to move: White announced double check and thought he would win easily, but Black mates.

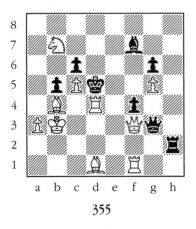

355

356

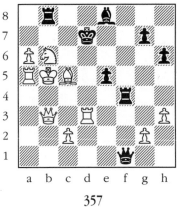

357

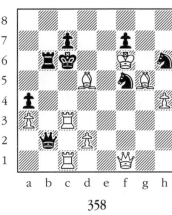

358

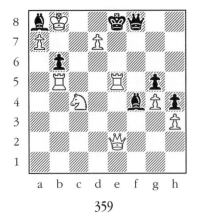

359

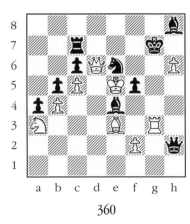

360

Pairs of Positions

The positions are similar but the solutions are different. White to move.

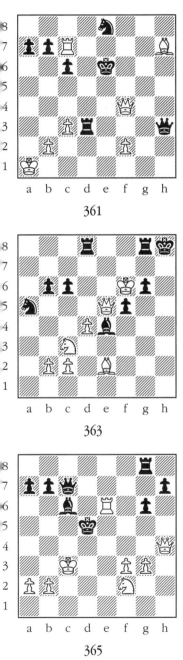

361

363

365

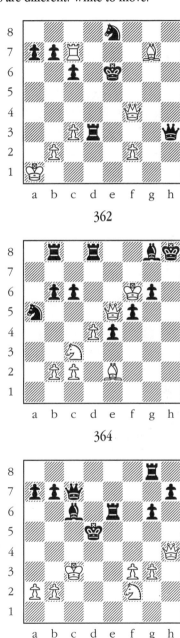

362

364

366

Pairs of Positions

The positions are similar but the solutions are different. Black to move.

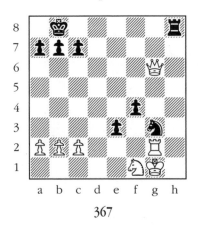

367

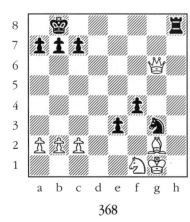

368

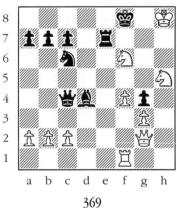

369

370

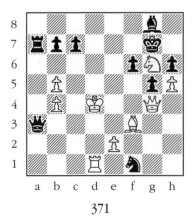

371

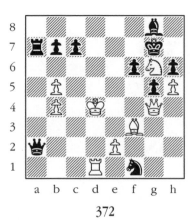

372

Pairs of Positions

The positions are similar but the solutions are different. White to move.

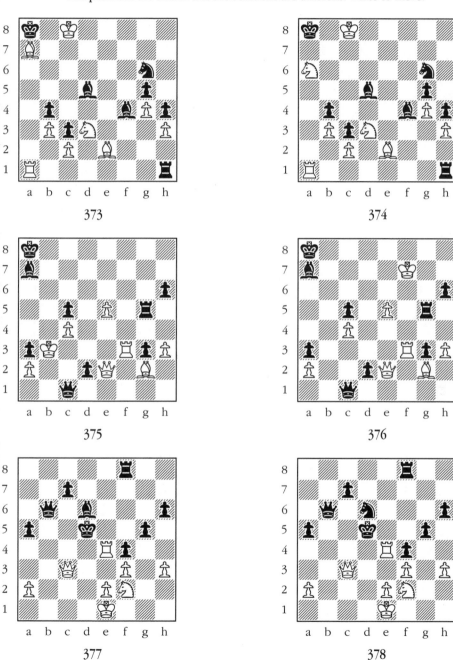

373

374

375

376

377

378

Pairs of Positions

The positions are similar but the solutions are different. Black to move.

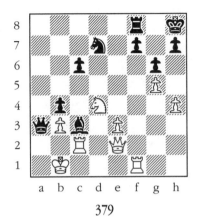

379

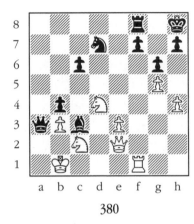

380

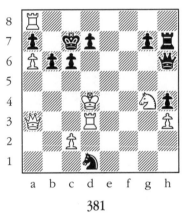

381

382

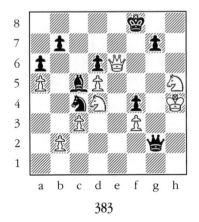

383

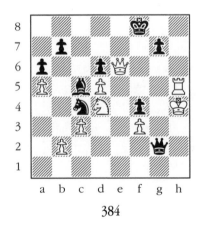

384

Pairs of Positions

The positions are similar but the solutions are different. White to move.

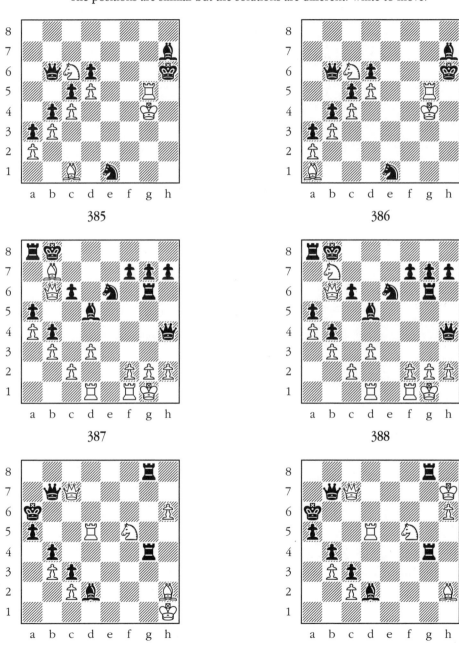

385

386

387

388

389

390

Mate in One in the Ending
Pawn Endings

White to move.

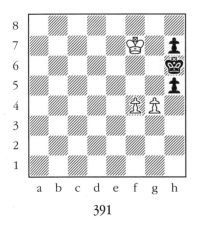

391

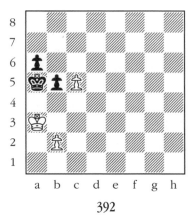

392

393

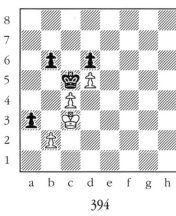

394

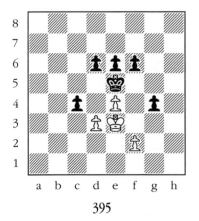

395

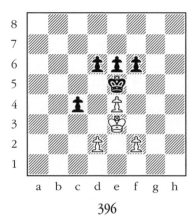

396

Pawn Endings

Black to move.

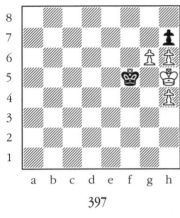

397

398

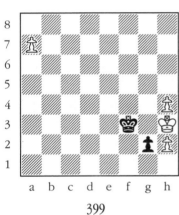

399

400

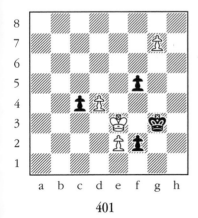

401

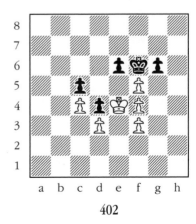

402

Minor-Piece Endings
Bishop Endings

White to move.

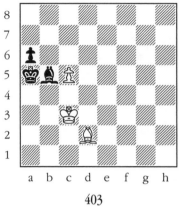

403

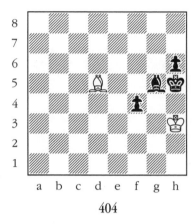

404

405

406

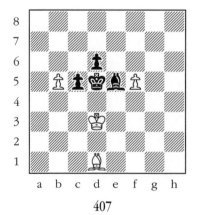

407

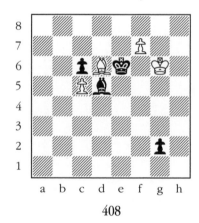

408

Bishop Endings

Black to move.

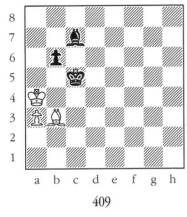

409

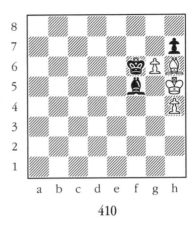

410

411

412

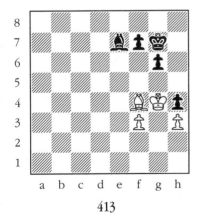

413

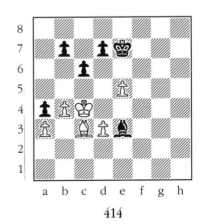

414

Knight Endings

White to move.

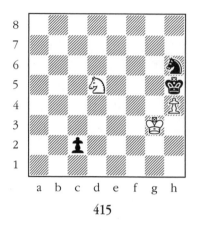

415

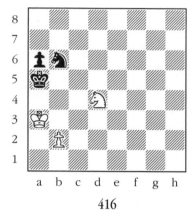

416

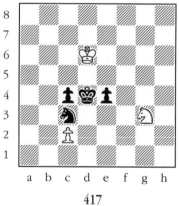

417

418

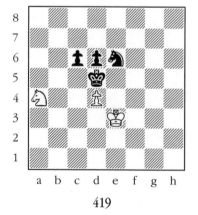

419

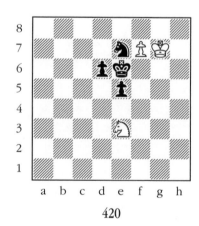

420

Knight Endings

Black to move.

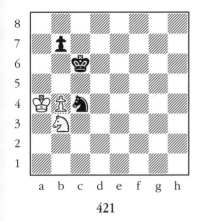

421

422

423

424

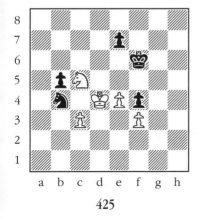

425

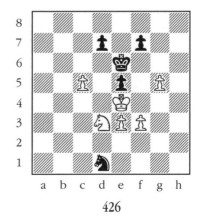

426

Four Knights

White to move.

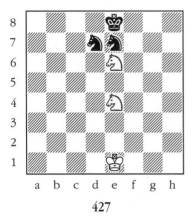

427

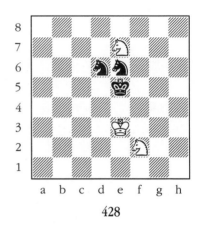

428

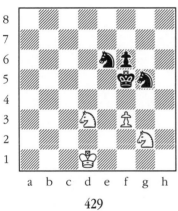

429

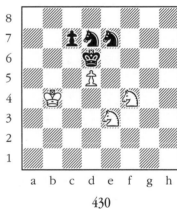

430

431

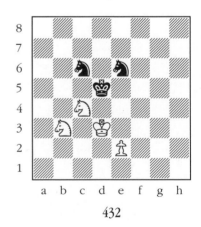

432

Four Bishops

White to move.

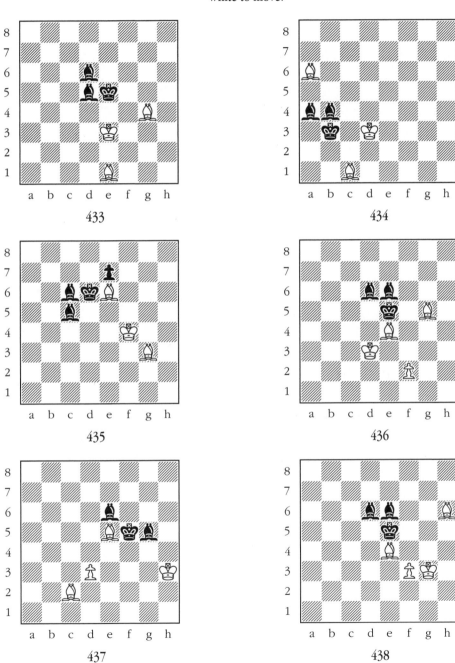

433

434

435

436

437

438

Bishop vs. Knight

White to move.

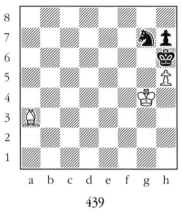

439

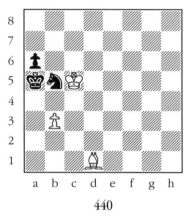

440

441

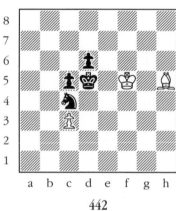

442

443

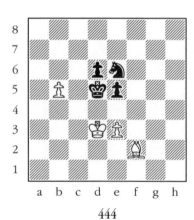

444

Knight vs. Bishop

White to move.

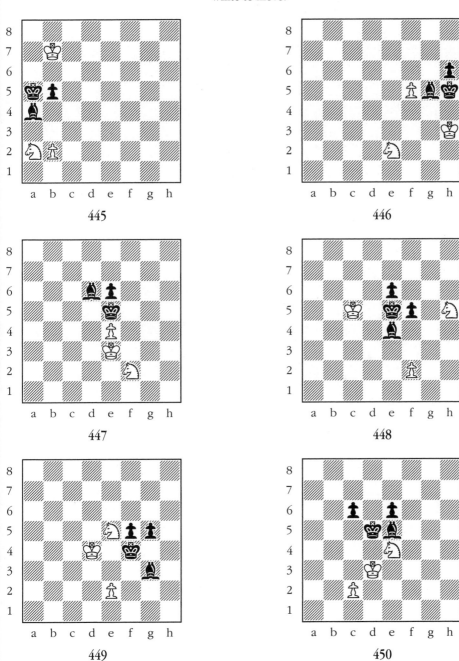

445

446

447

448

449

450

Two Bishops vs. Two Knights

White to move.

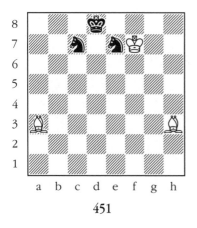

451

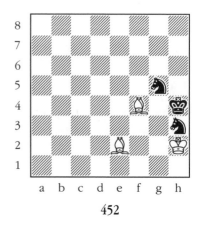

452

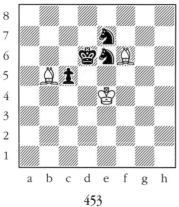

453

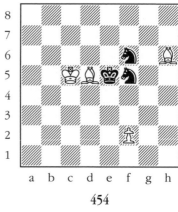

454

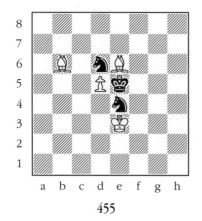

455

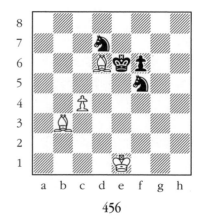

456

Two Knights vs. Two Bishops

Black to move.

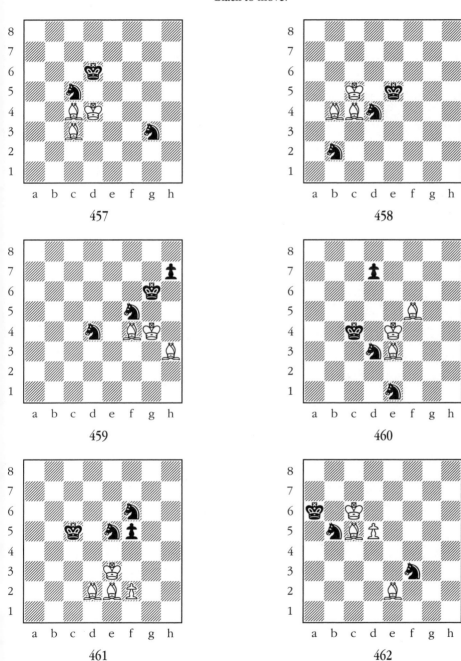

457

458

459

460

461

462

Bishop and Knight vs. Bishop and Knight

White to move.

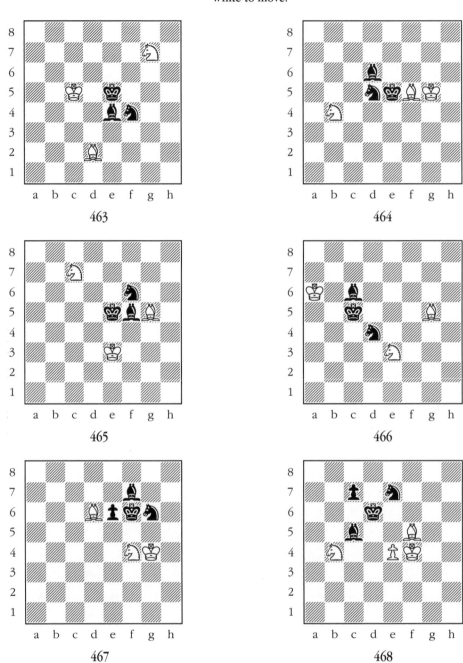

463

464

465

466

467

468

Major Piece vs. Minor Piece
Rook vs. Knight

White to move.

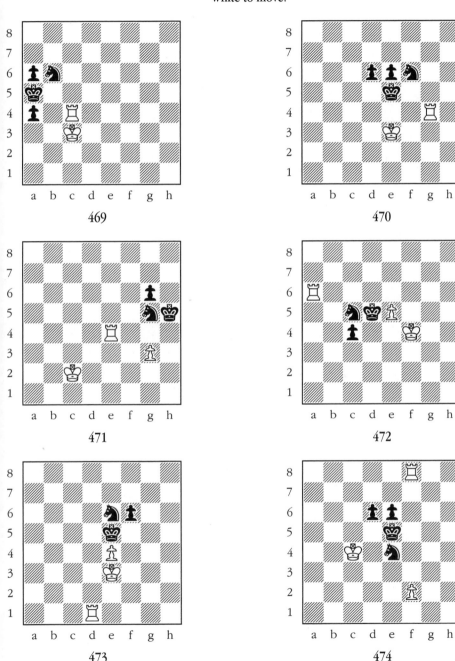

469

470

471

472

473

474

Rook vs. Bishop

Black to move.

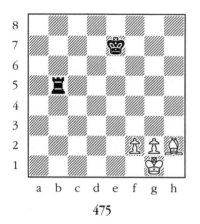

475

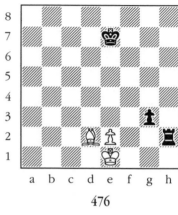

476

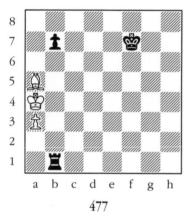

477

478

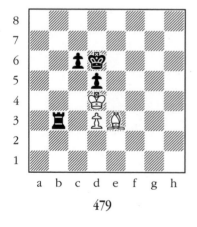

479

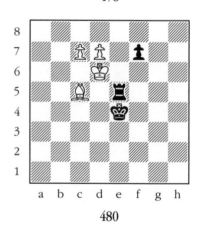

480

Major-Piece Endings
Rook Endings

White to move.

481

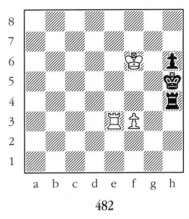

482

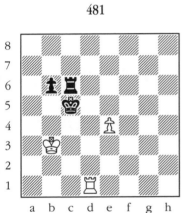

483

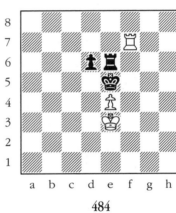

484

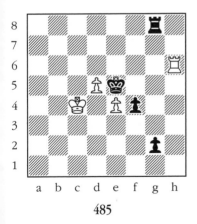

485

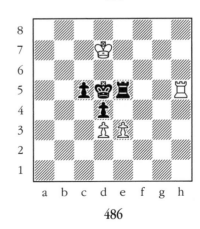

486

Rook Endings

Black to move.

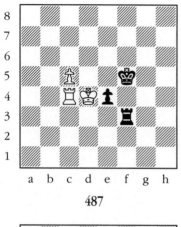

487

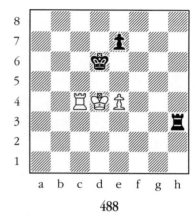

488

489

490

491

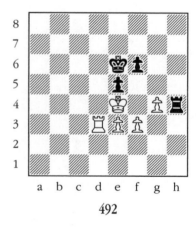

492

Queen Endings

White to move.

493

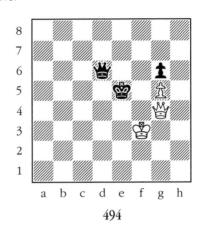

494

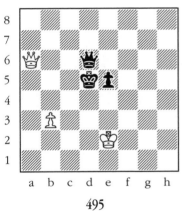

495

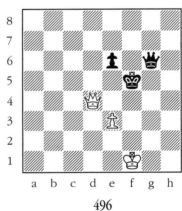

496

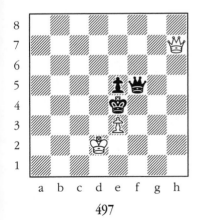

497

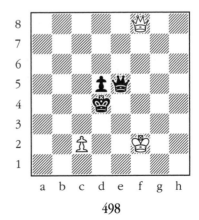

498

Queen Endings

Black to move.

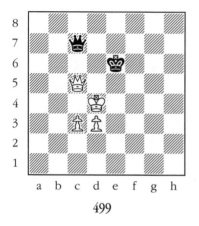

499

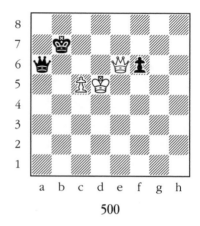

500

501

502

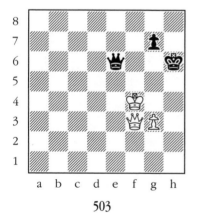

503

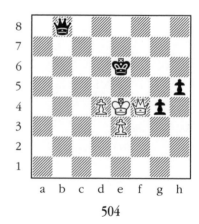

504

90

Four Rooks

Black to move.

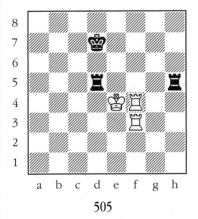

505

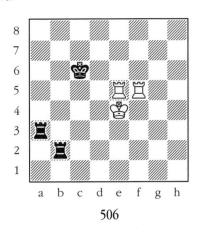

506

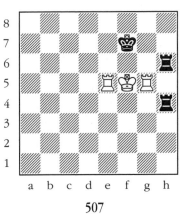

507

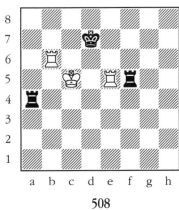

508

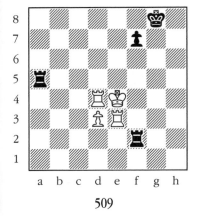

509

510

Pairs of Positions

The positions are similar but the solutions are different. Black to move.

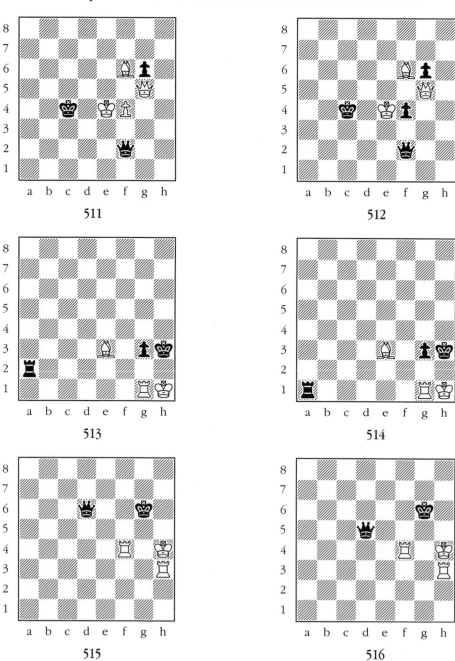

511

512

513

514

515

516

Pairs of Positions

The positions are similar but the solutions are different. White to move.

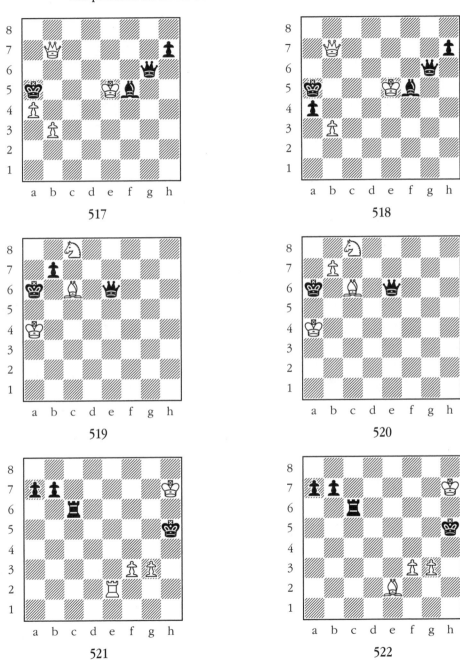

517

518

519

520

521

522

Pairs of Positions

The positions are similar but the solutions are different. Black to move.

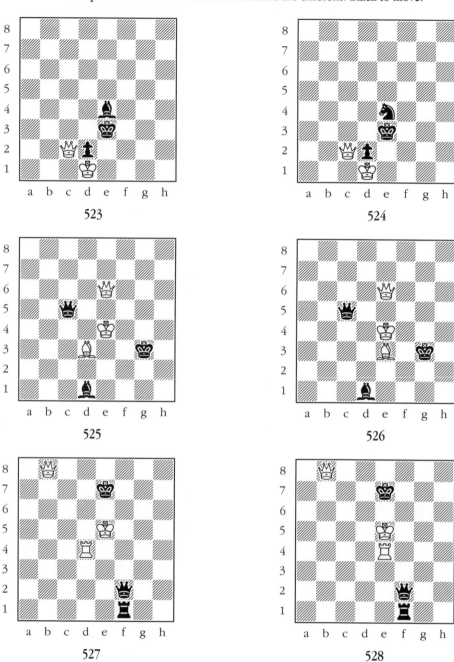

523

524

525

526

527

528

Pairs of Positions

The positions are similar but the solutions are different. White to move.

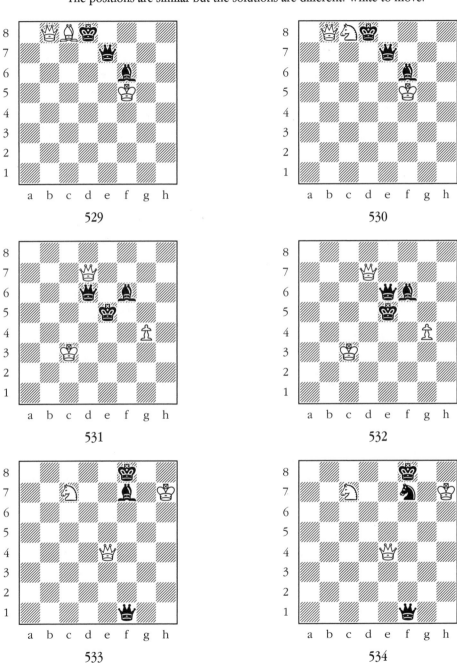

529

530

531

532

533

534

Pairs of Positions

The positions are similar but the solutions are different. Black to move.

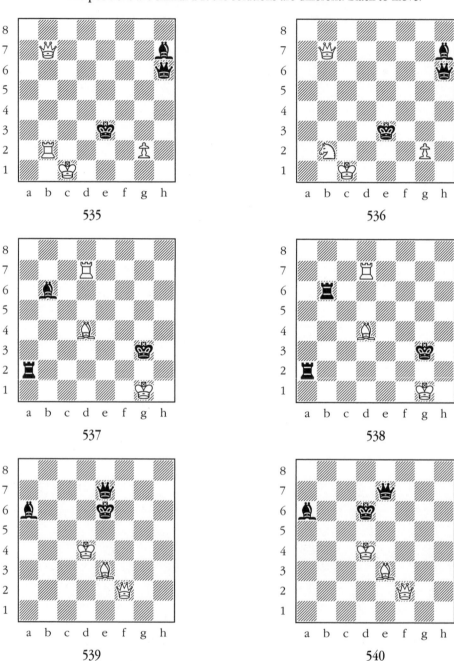

535

536

537

538

539

540

Pairs of Positions

The positions are similar but the solutions are different. White to move.

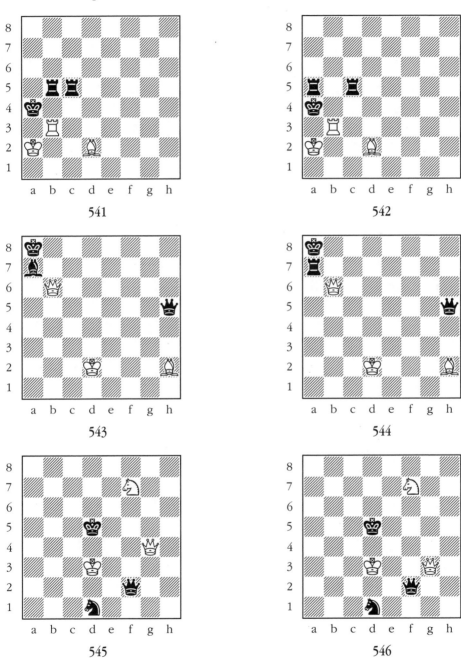

541

542

543

544

545

546

Pairs of Positions

The positions are similar but the solutions are different. Black to move.

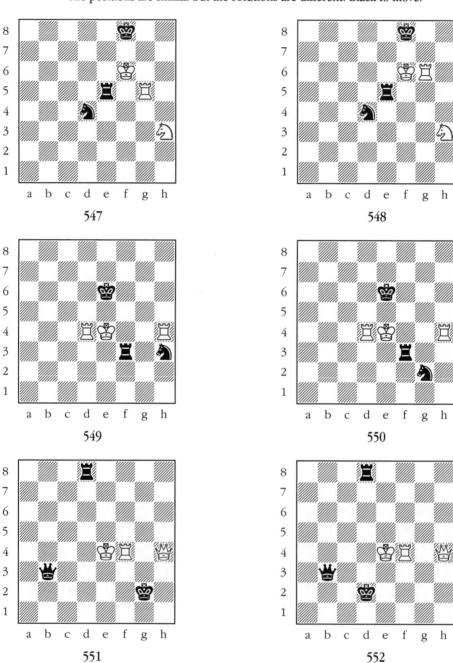

547

548

549

550

551

552

Pairs of Positions

The positions are similar but the solutions are different. Black to move.

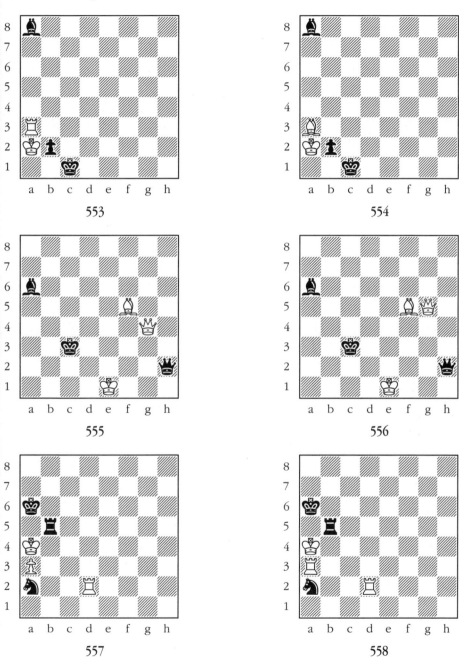

553

554

555

556

557

558

Chess Aesthetics
All the Pieces on the Same Diagonal

White to move.

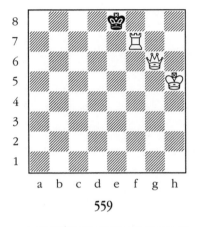

559

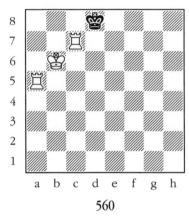

560

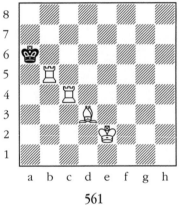

561

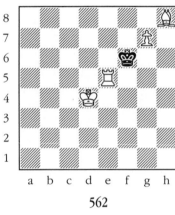

562

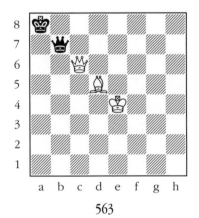

563

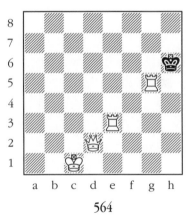

564

All the Pieces on the Long Diagonal

White to move — two solutions.

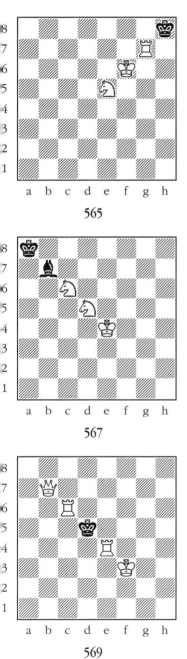

565

567

569

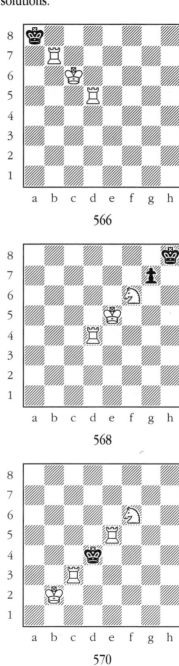

566

568

570

All the Pieces on the Same File

White to move.

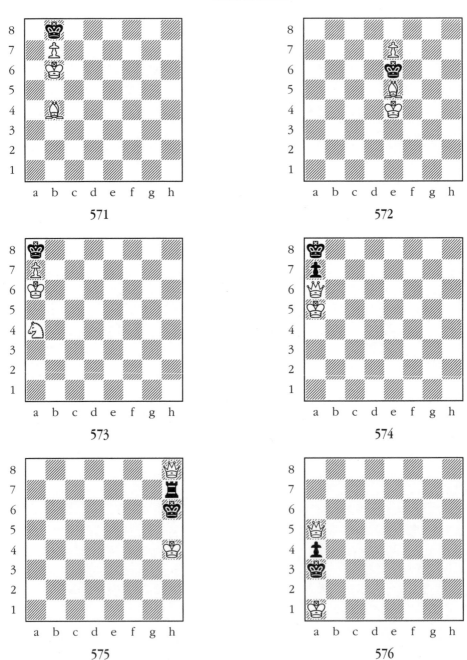

571

572

573

574

575

576

All the Pieces on the Same File

White to move.

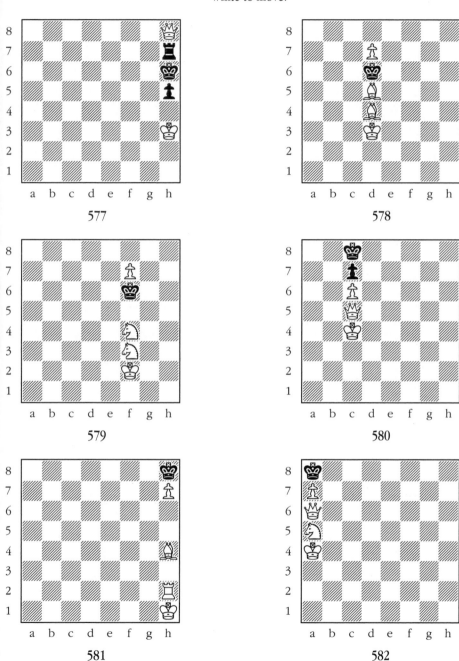

577

578

579

580

581

582

All the Pieces on the Same File

Black to move.

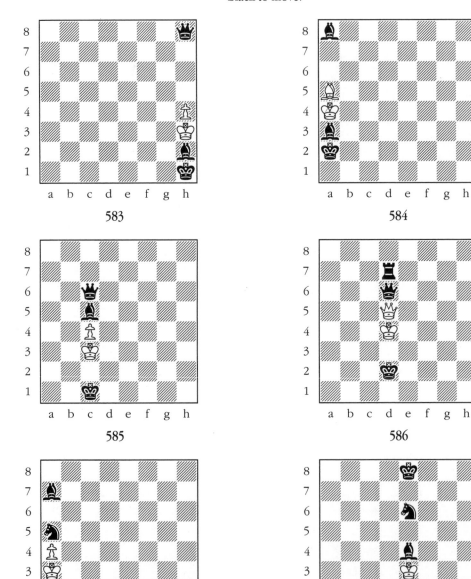

583

584

585

586

587

588

All the Pieces on the Same Rank

White to move.

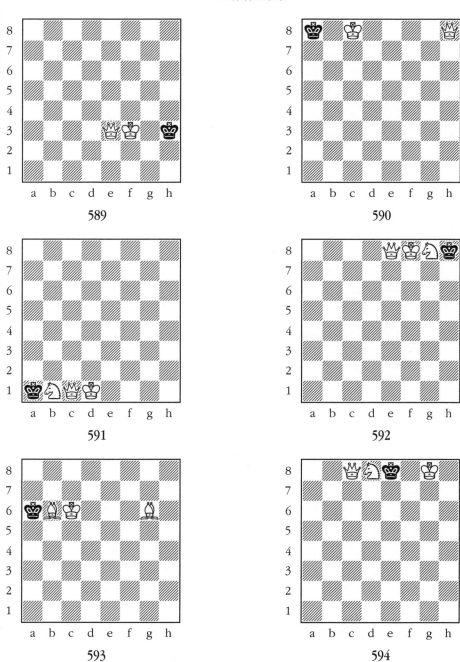

589

590

591

592

593

594

All the Pieces on the Same Rank

White to move.

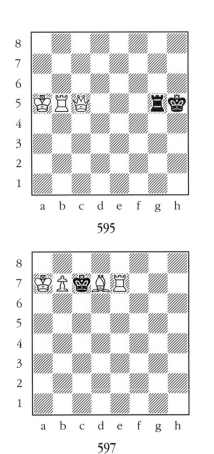

595

596

597

598

599

600

All the Pieces on the Same Rank

Black to move.

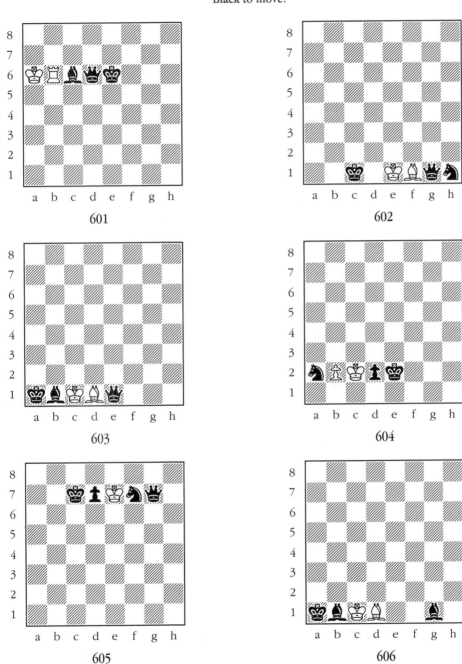

601

602

603

604

605

606

All the Pieces on the Same Rank

White to move.

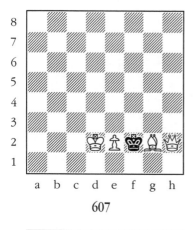

607

608

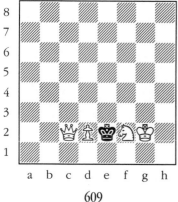

609

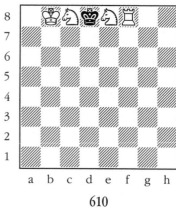

610

611

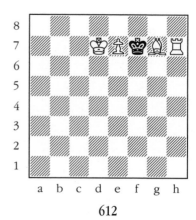

612

All the Pieces on the Same Rank

White to move.

613

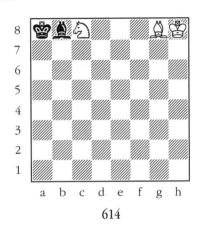

614

615

616

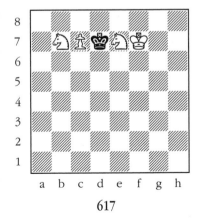

617

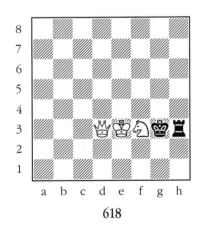

618

Solutions

1. 1. ♕h5#.
2. 1. ♗xg6#.
3. 1. ♗h5#.
4. 1. ♘f6#.
5. 1. ♘d6#.
6. 1. ♕xg6#.
7. 1...bxc1♕#.
8. 1...♖xc1#.
9. 1...♕xc1#.
10. 1...♖xh1#.
11. 1...c1♕#.
12. 1...♘xc2#.
13. 1. ♕(♗)xf7#.
14. 1. ♕(♗)xf7#.
15. 1. ♕(♗)xf7#.
16. 1. exf7(gxf7)#.
17. 1. ♕xf7(gxf7)#.
18. 1. ♗xf7(exf7)#.
19. 1...♕xf2#.
20. 1...♗xf2#.
21. 1...♕xf2#.
22. 1...♕xf2#.
23. 1...♗xf2#.
24. 1...♗xf2#.
25. 1. c3#.
26. 1. c4#.
27. 1. ♘c3#.
28. 1. ♘f3#.
29. 1. g3#.
30. 1. d4#.
31. 1...e5#.
32. 1...e6#.
33. 1...h5#.
34. 1...♘f6#.
35. 1...♘a6#.
36. 1...e6#.
37. 1...♕g3#.
38. 1...♗g3#.
39. 1...♕xe4#.

40. 1...♘d3#.
41. 1...♕xd4#.
42. 1...♕xc1#.
43. 1. ♕g6#.
44. 1. ♕g6#.
45. 1. ♗h5#.
46. 1. ♗g6#.
47. 1. ♕h5#.
48. 1. ♕h5#.
49. 1...♕b4#.
50. 1...♕xd4#.
51. 1...♕f4#.
52. 1...♕g4#.
53. 1...♕d4#.
54. 1...♕xf4#.
55. 1. ♕xc8#.
56. 1. ♕xc8#.
57. 1. ♕xd8#.
58. 1. ♘d6#.
59. 1. f7#.
60. 1. ♖xh8#.
61. 1. ♕xe5#.
62. 1. ♕xf7#.
63. 1. ♕xf8#.
64. 1. ♕g5#.
65. 1. g5#.
66. 1. ♕h5#.
67. 1...♕xf1#.
68. 1...♘xc2#.
69. 1...♘xf2#.
70. 1...♕xe2#.
71. 1...♖e1#.
72. 1...♕xc1#.
73. 1. ♘f6#.
74. 1. ♕d5#.
75. 1. ♕b5#.
76. 1. gxh8♘#.
77. 1. ♘f7#.
78. 1. ♗h6#.

79. 1...♕xe4#.
80. 1...♕xe3#.
81. 1...♗h3#.
82. 1...♗h3#.
83. 1...♕e1#.
84. 1...g2#.
85. 1. ♕e5#.
86. 1. ♕xd8#.
87. 1. ♕xg7#.
88. 1. ♖d8#.
89. 1. ♘f7#.
90. 1. ♖h8#.
91. 1. ♕d8#.
92. 1. ♕xf7#.
93. 1. ♕xg7#.
94. 1. ♕xg7#.
95. 1. ♗xf6#.
96. 1. ♕xh7#.
97. 1. ♕xf7#.
98. 1. ♕xf8#.
99. 1. ♗g5#.
100. 1. ♖e8#.
101. 1. f7#.
102. 1. ♗e8#.
103. 1. ♘f6#.
104. 1. ♕d5#.
105. 1. ♕f8#.
106. 1. ♘xg6#.
107. 1. ♘xg6#.
108. 1. ♗xf7#.
109. 1...d5#.
110. 1...♘c5#.
111. 1...♕h1#.
112. 1...♖d1#.
113. 1...♕g3#.
114. 1...♗h3#.
115. 1. ♕xe5#.
116. 1. ♕xg8#.
117. 1. ♕f5#.

118. 1. ♕xg5#.
119. 1. ♕f7#.
120. 1. hxg5#.
121. 1. ♕f7#.
122. 1. ♗e3#.
123. 1. ♕xe6#.
124. 1. ♘xb5#.
125. 1. ♕xd6#.
126. 1. ♘xe6#.
127. 1...♘xf2#.
128. 1...♖e1#.
129. 1...♗g4#.
130. 1...♕xe2#.
131. 1...♕xg2#.
132. 1...♘f2#.
133. 1. ♘d5#.
134. 1. ♕e6#.
135. 1. ♕e8#.
136. 1. ♕f5#.
137. 1. exf7#.
138. 1. ♘c3#.
139. 1. ♕xf7#.
140. 1. ♘g6#.
141. 1. ♗g5#.
142. 1. ♗f7#.
143. 1. ♕e8#.
144. 1. ♖d6#.
145. 1. ♘f6#.
146. 1. ♕xh8#.
147. 1. ♗h6#.
148. 1. ♕xe7#.
149. 1. ♕g8#.
150. 1. ♕f7#.
151. 1. ♕xf7#.
152. 1. ♗e6#.
153. 1. ♕xh7#.
154. 1. ♕f5#.
155. 1. ♕xe7#.
156. 1. ♕a8#.

157. 1. Bg5#.	198. 1...Nxh3#.	239. 1. Qb3#.	280. 1...h5#.
158. 1. Nf7#.	199. 1. Bxd7#.	240. 1. Ba6#.	281. 1...Nxb4#.
159. 1. Nf7#.	200. 1. bxa8Q(R)#.	241. 1. Qf3#.	282. 1...Qe3#.
160. 1. b4#.	201. 1. Nxc7#.	242. 1. Qh3#.	283. 1...Bxf2#.
161. 1. Be3#.	202. 1. Nxd6#.	243. 1. Qc3#.	284. 1...Nc2#.
162. 1. Nd6#.	203. 1. Qxe6#.	244. 1. Qg3#.	285. 1...Nf3#.
163. 1...Ng3#.	204. 1. dxc6#.	245. 1. Nd5#.	286. 1...Nd3#.
164. 1...Rd1#.	205. 1...Qe4#.	246. 1. Qc8#.	287. 1...Qg6#.
165. 1...b4#.	206. 1...Bg4#.	247. 1. Qf5#.	288. 1...Bxf3#.
166. 1...Nxh3#.	207. 1...Qd2#.	248. 1. Qd5#.	289. 1. Qxa7#.
167. 1...Qe7#.	208. 1...Bb4#.	249. 1. Bxf7#.	290. 1. Qf8#.
168. 1...Ng2#.	209. 1...Bf5#.	250. 1. Bf7#.	291. 1. b7#.
169. 1. Qxh7#.	210. 1...Bc5#.	251. 1. g7#.	292. 1. Rf8#.
170. 1. Qh8#.	211. 1. Bxg6#.	252. 1. Bg6#.	293. 1. Qf5#.
171. 1. Qf8#.	212. 1. exf7#.	253. 1...Qh4#.	294. 1. Rg8#.
172. 1. d5#.	213. 1. Qd5#.	254. 1...Qg3#.	295. 1...Bb2#.
173. 1. Qf6#.	214. 1. Qc8#.	255. 1...Ng3#.	296. 1...Bf6#.
174. 1. Nc4#.	215. 1. Bg5#.	256. 1...Qh3#.	297. 1...Nf2#.
175. 1...Nf2#.	216. 1. Re8#.	257. 1...Qh2#.	298. 1...c2#.
176. 1...Ng3#.	217. 1...Nd3#.	258. 1...0-0#.	299. 1...Qxh4#.
177. 1...Bxe4#.	218. 1...Nd3#.	259. 1...Bg3#.	300. 1...Qxd3#.
178. 1...Bxf3#.	219. 1...Nd4#.	260. 1...Qxg3#.	301. 1. Rxd5#.
179. 1...Nd4#.	220. 1...Bh3#.	261. 1...Qxh4#.	302. 1. Qd4#.
180. 1...gxh2#.	221. 1...Qg2#.	262. 1...Qxd4#.	303. 1. Bxd4#.
181. 1. Qxf7#.	222. 1...Nh3#.	263. 1...Bf2#.	304. 1. Qxe5#.
182. 1. Qf8#.	223. 1. Nf6#.	264. 1...Bg4#.	305. 1. Bxe6#.
183. 1. Nf6#.	224. 1. Nd6#.	265. 1. Qh5#.	306. 1. Qc3xd4#.
184. 1. Rxe8#.	225. 1. Qf8#.	266. 1. Bg6#.	307. 1. Nxd6#.
185. 1. Q(R)e8#.	226. 1. Qh7#.	267. 1. Ng6#.	308. 1. Rxa5#.
186. 1. Qf8#.	227. 1. Qh3#.	268. 1. Ne6#.	309. 1. Ba5#.
187. 1. Qxd7#.	228. 1. Qh7#.	269. 1. Qh5#.	310. 1. Nxf6#.
188. 1. exd8Q(R)#.	229. 1...Qxe4#.	270. 1. Bf7#.	311. 1. bxc6#.
189. 1. Bb5#.	230. 1...Qxh2#.	271. 1. Nc7#.	312. 1. Rxh2#.
190. 1. f7#.	231. 1...Qd3#.	272. 1. Bg5#.	313. 1...Nxf2#.
191. 1. Qd7#.	232. 1...Bb4#.	273. 1. Nc7#.	314. 1...Nf5#.
192. 1. e7#.	233. 1...Qxh2#.	274. 1. Bg5#.	315. 1...Be5#.
193. 1...Qh1#.	234. 1...Nxf2#.	275. 1. Qe5#.	316. 1...Nxd4#.
194. 1...Qh4#.	235. 1. Nxf6#.	276. 1. Ne7#.	317. 1...Nf3#.
195. 1...Ne2#.	236. 1. Nd6#.	277. 1...Nd3#.	318. 1...fxe5#.
196. 1...Qh6#.	237. 1. Qxg6#.	278. 1...Qe4#.	319. 1. f7#.
197. 1...hxg4#.	238. 1. Bd8#.	279. 1...Qh4#.	320. 1. Ng1#.

321. 1. exf6#.	362. 1. ♕e5#.	403. 1. ♔b3#.	444. 1. e4#.
322. 1. ♗g7#.	363. 1. ♕h2#.	404. 1. ♗f7#.	445. 1. b4#.
323. 1. ♗c5#.	364. 1. ♔xg6#.	405. 1. ♗f3#.	446. 1. ♘g3#.
324. 1. axb5#.	365. 1. ♕c4#.	406. 1. d4#.	447. 1. ♘g4#.
325. 1...♘f3#.	366. 1. ♕d4#.	407. 1. ♗f3#.	448. 1. f4#.
326. 1...d4#.	367. 1...♖h1#.	408. 1. f8♘#.	449. 1. e3#.
327. 1...♖c1#.	368. 1...♘e2#.	409. 1...b5#.	450. 1. c4#.
328. 1...♗f2#.	369. 1...♕g8#.	410. 1...hxg6#.	451. 1. ♗xe7#.
329. 1...♖xf2#.	370. 1...♕xh5#.	411. 1...d1♕#.	452. 1. ♗g3#.
330. 1...♖h3#.	371. 1...♕e3#.	412. 1...♗g6#.	453. 1. ♗e5#.
331. 1...♕h2#.	372. 1...♕c4#.	413. 1...f5#.	454. 1. f4#.
332. 1...♕g2#.	373. 1. ♗g1#.	414. 1...b5#.	455. 1. ♗d4#.
333. 1...♕h1#.	374. 1. ♘c7#.	415. 1. ♘f4#.	456. 1. c5#.
334. 1...♕xh2#.	375. 1. ♖f8#.	416. 1. b4#.	457. 1...♘f5#.
335. 1...♖h1#.	376. 1. ♖b3#.	417. 1. ♘f5#.	458. 1...♘a4#.
336. 1...♗h2#.	377. 1. ♕c4#.	418. 1. ♘c4#.	459. 1...h5#.
337. 1...♕xb7#.	378. 1. ♖e5#.	419. 1. ♘b6#.	460. 1...d5#.
338. 1...♕b7#.	379. 1...♕a1#.	420. 1. f8♘#.	461. 1...♘d5#.
339. 1. ♗a6#.	380. 1...♕b2#.	421. 1...b5#.	462. 1...♘e5#.
340. 1. ♘xa6#.	381. 1...♕f4#.	422. 1...♘f5#.	463. 1. ♗c3#.
341. 1. ♕xb6#.	382. 1...♕d5#.	423. 1...♘g2#.	464. 1. ♘c6#.
342. 1. ♘de7#.	383. 1...g5#.	424. 1...c5#.	465. 1. ♗f4#.
343. 1. ♗xg6#.	384. 1...♕g3#.	425. 1...e5#.	466. 1. ♗e7#.
344. 1. ♗xb5#.	385. 1. ♖g8#.	426. 1...♘c3#.	467. 1. ♘h5#.
345. 1. ♗xd7#.	386. 1. ♗g7#.	427. 1. ♘d6#.	468. 1. e5#.
346. 1. ♖d8#.	387. 1. ♗a6#.	428. 1. ♘g4#.	469. 1. ♖c5#.
347. 1. ♕xe6#.	388. 1. ♘d6#.	429. 1. ♘h4#.	470. 1. ♖g5#.
348. 1. ♕xe7#.	389. 1. ♕xa5#.	430. 1. ♘c4#.	471. 1. ♖h4#.
349. 1. ♗xb7#.	390. 1. ♖xa5#.	431. 1. ♘g3#.	472. 1. ♖d6#.
350. 1. ♗c1#.	391. 1. g5#.	432. 1. e4#.	473. 1. ♖d5#.
351. 1. ♖xf2#.	392. 1. b4#.	433. 1. ♗c3#.	474. 1. f4#.
352. 1. ♗f1#.	393. 1. g4#.	434. 1. ♗c4#.	475. 1...♖b1#.
353. 1. ♕xd2#.	394. 1. b4#.	435. 1. ♔f5#.	476. 1...♖h1#.
354. 1. d4#.	395. 1. d4#.	436. 1. f4#.	477. 1...b5#.
355. 1...♔xd4#.	396. 1. f4#.	437. 1. d4#.	478. 1...f5#.
356. 1...♔e8#.	397. 1...hxg6#.	438. 1. ♗g7#.	479. 1...c5#.
357. 1...♔c7#.	398. 1...b5#.	439. 1. ♗c1#.	480. 1...♖e6#.
358. 1...♔xd5#.	399. 1...g1♘#.	440. 1. b4#.	481. 1. ♖a4#.
359. 1...♔xd7#.	400. 1...e5#.	441. 1. ♗g4#.	482. 1. ♖e5#.
360. 1...♔f7#.	401. 1...f1♘#.	442. 1. ♗f3#.	483. 1. ♖d5#.
361. 1. ♗g8#.	402. 1...gxf5#.	443. 1. d8♘#.	484. 1. ♖f5#.

485. 1. ♖e6#.

486. 1. e4#.

487. 1... ♖d3#.

488. 1...e5#.

489. 1... ♖e1#.

490. 1... ♖e7#.

491. 1... ♖e8#.

492. 1...f5#.

493. 1. b7#.

494. 1. ♕e4#.

495. 1. ♕c4#.

496. 1. ♕f4#.

497. 1. ♕b7#.

498. 1. ♕b4#.

499. 1...♕f4#.

500. 1...♕d3#.

501. 1...♕f3#.

502. 1...♕c3#.

503. 1...g5#.

504. 1...♕b1#.

505. 1... ♖he5#.

506. 1... ♖b4#.

507. 1... ♖f6#.

508. 1... ♖xe5#.

509. 1...f5#.

510. 1... ♖d5#.

511. 1...♕e2#.

512. 1...♕e3#.

513. 1... ♖h2#.

514. 1...g2#.

515. 1...♕xf4#.

516. 1...♕g5#.

517. 1. ♕b5#.

518. 1. b4#.

519. 1. ♗b5#.

520. 1. b8♘#.

521. 1. ♖e5#.

522. 1. f4#.

523. 1... ♗f3#.

524. 1...♘f2#.

525. 1...♗f3#.

526. 1...♗c2#.

527. 1...♕f5#.

528. 1...♕c5#.

529. 1. ♗e6#.

530. 1. ♘b6#.

531. 1. ♕f5#.

532. 1. ♕d4#.

533. 1. ♕b4#.

534. 1. ♕e8#.

535. 1...♕h1#.

536. 1...♔e2#.

537. 1... ♖a1#.

538. 1... ♖b1#.

539. 1...♕b4#.

540. 1...♕e5#.

541. 1. ♖a3#.

542. 1. ♖b4#.

543. 1. ♕c6#.

544. 1. ♕b8#.

545. 1. ♕c4#.

546. 1. ♕d6#.

547. 1. ♖e6#.

548. 1. ♖f5#.

549. 1...♘g5#.

550. 1... ♖e3#.

551. 1...♕e6#.

552. 1...♕d5#.

553. 1...b1♕#.

554. 1...♗d5#.

555. 1...♕d2#.

556. 1...♕e2#.

557. 1...♘c3#.

558. 1... ♖b4#.

559. 1...♕g8#.

560. 1. ♖a8#.

561. 1. ♖a4#.

562. 1. g8♕#.

563. 1. ♕xb7#.

564. 1. ♖h3#.

565. 1. ♘f7(g6)#.

566. 1. ♖a5(d8)#.

567. 1. ♘b6(c7)#.

568. 1. ♖d8(h4)#.

569. 1. ♕b5(d7)#.

570. 1. ♖d5(e4)#.

571. 1. ♗d6#.

572. 1. e8♕#.

573. 1. ♘b6#.

574. 1. ♕c8#.

575. 1. ♕f6#.

576. 1. ♕c3#.

577. 1. ♕f6#.

578. 1. d8♕#.

579. 1. f8♕#.

580. 1. ♕f8#.

581. 1. ♗f6#.

582. 1. ♕b7#.

583. 1...♕c8#.

584. 1...♗c6#.

585. 1...♕f3#.

586. 1...♕xd5#.

587. 1...♗c5#.

588. 1...e1♕#.

589. 1. ♕h6#.

590. 1. ♕a1#.

591. 1. ♘c3#.

592. 1. ♕h5#.

593. 1. ♗d3#.

594. 1. ♘c6#.

595. 1. ♕xg5#.

596. 1. ♕a8#.

597. 1. b8♕#.

598. 1. d8♕#.

599. 1. d8♕#.

600. 1. e5#.

601. 1...♕a3#.

602. 1...♕f2#.

603. 1...♕e3#.

604. 1...d1♕#.

605. 1...♘d6#.

606. 1...♗e3#.

607. 1. ♗h3#.

608. 1. ♕d4#.

609. 1. ♕d1#.

610. 1. ♘f6#.

611. 1. d8♕#.

612. 1. e8♕#.

613. 1. ♕e2#.

614. 1. ♗d5#.

615. 1. ♗c6#.

616. 1. ♘c3#.

617. 1. c8♕#.

618. 1. ♕g6#.